The Apocalypse Survival Guide to Bugging In & Home Defense

Steve Rayder

Steve Rayder

www.southshorepublications.com

© 2015 by SouthShore Publications & Distribution.

ISBN- 978-1512007091

ISBN-10: 1512007099

CONTENTS

1. INTRODUCTION

If a breakdown of modern society were to occur, do we stay where we are and bug in for the long haul or do we leave our homes and bug out to a different location?

In a 'without rule of law' or WROL situation it seems that a lot of preppers will choose to bug out and get away from civilization as soon as possible. But in this book I'm going to give you my thoughts on why bugging is a much better idea.

Now I'm not saying don't be prepared to bug out. You should keep a bug out bag for when and if you do need to leave your home. Because you never know if you will have to leave in a hurry at some point. But what if your home gets destroyed or is made uninhabitable? This could be caused by severe flooding, fire, an earthquake or even a chemical, biological or nuclear attack in the vicinity of your home.

In all of those scenarios you would need to leave and bug out. But why do it any sooner than you need to? There are so many benefits to staying in the safety and comfort of your home for as long as possible.

2. WHERE WOULD YOU GO ANYWAY?

Perhaps the biggest factor that makes me think bugging in is the best idea is this one simple thing. If you were to leave, where would you even go?

Most people will say, "I'm going out into the woods and I'm going to survive off the land." Well that's the problem right there, most people will say that. So you and over 50% of the population are all going into the woods at the same time.

You will be very hard pressed to find an area where other people aren't going to stumble across your camp unless you're setting up a shelter on top of a mountain.

Also, there will be large groups out there, and without rule of law, they will be laying claim to areas of forest and open land where they can grow crops and hunt without other people stealing it from them and they will defend that land. So if you think you're going to be able to just come along and hunt on their patch then you're going to run into trouble.

Also, you can be prepared to live out in the woods but if you haven't actually tried it, then it will probably be a lot harder than you think. If that genuinely is your plan, you should go out into the woods with no food or water and see how long you can survive. If you can do it then you're one of the few with the skills necessary.

Even if you can, you still have to find an area where no one else will be, and if no one else is there, there's probably a pretty good reason for that.

On top of this, everyone else is going to be out there hunting for any kind of wildlife they can find so there will be huge culls of every type of animal right away. So you will be very hard pressed to find enough to feed yourself and anyone else you're with.

Your best bet for bugging out is to have an established bug out location in as much of a remote area as you can possibly find. Make a decent shelter there and stockpile supplies. That way at least you will have food for a while as long as it's not discovered and looted.

Water is another concern. Obviously the forest is generally a much better place to find water than an urban area as there will be streams and rivers that you can camp close to. But, everyone else who is going to the forest to bug out is also going to want to be close to a river or stream. So by setting up close to a water source you are massively increasing your chance of being discovered.

There are of course variables depending on your location. For example if you live in a very unpopulated region then the land around you should stay fairly free of outsiders for a time. Although if the situation continues for long enough, with everyone leaving urban areas in search of food and animals to hunt, even the most remote areas will start to get visitors.

You could also have a particularly good bug out location that would make your chances of survival in the wild more appealing. For example, you could set up camp a small island the middle of a lake or river. This would make it far less likely that people would stumble across you randomly. But if someone else has the same idea, which they probably will, they might try and get to the island too.

So all of this leads me to the conclusion that seeing as there isn't really going to be anywhere to go, you should stay put while you can.

3. OTHER SURVIVORS

Another reason to stay in your home is that by leaving, you are greatly increasing the chance you will encounter other survivors. You don't know these people and you don't know if they are the sort of person who will attack you or take your supplies from you.

I don't want anyone to think I'm being over dramatic here, but human history has shown us that a lot people have no problem stealing what they need from other people. It's that simple.

Hunger drives people to do things they would never normally do, especially if their family is starving to death for example. Ask yourself this, if you saw another survivor walking around and you noticed he had food but he wouldn't give you any, and you had a child at home that was dying of starvation would you take at least some of it from him if you could?

Many people would probably answer yes to that question. So it's not even necessarily evil people who will attack you or steal from you, just desperate people.

The strongest and the smartest will survive. There will be no room for weakness. In these circumstances you don't want to be bumping into other people that you don't know. On the road you will be doing just that.

By staying at home you will not only decrease the chance of running into people like this, you will also give yourself a better chance of defending yourself.

Or even having other people to help you defend against them. Because they won't just be trying to raid your house, they will be raiding your neighbor's houses too and you're not all just going to stand by and let it happen are you?

The chances are these raiding groups won't be large and well organized, more likely a group of jumped up bullies who are far too big for their boots and just going round thinking they can take what they want from anyone.

What you will have is a community of people who have no choice but to defend themselves and they will do so together in an organized way. You will also have the home advantage. When it's on your turf you can set up defenses and dictate the rules and you will know the layout of the area and the buildings better than them giving you the advantage.

If these looters encounter a strong resistance from a neighborhood they will just move on to the next one. I doubt it would even come to a confrontation. If they saw a group of people closing off your road, even with primitive weaponry, it's doubtful they would even bother giving it a second thought. They would most likely move on to weaker targets who can't defend themselves quite so well.

However, if you're out with just a few other people in the woods, it will be much harder to defend yourself to say the least. You will have no walls to hide behind if you need to and you will have fewer neighbors or a smaller community to help you if thing come to a head and to help keep watch.

Steve Rayder

4. YOUR NEIGHBORS

So as I just mentioned, without rule of law you will probably want to form a neighborhood support system of some kind. For example if you live in a block of flats you could all get together and form a plan of how to defend the building from looters and go on supply runs together. The same thing goes for a street of houses.

Of course, you may not get on with or trust your neighbors so you may feel that this could be a risky strategy. In most cases it will be much better than trying to go it alone. Just remember that ultimately everyone will be out for themselves.

If you do decide to go it alone then keep in mind that without rule of law for a long enough amount of time, looking at the history of humanity and generally just taking into account about what we know of human nature in general, you will probably need to defend yourself at some point.

Of course there will be good people out there too, so if there are people you know quite well and that can trust not to stab you in the back at the first chance they get then join up with them. By bugging in and staying at home, you will obviously have a much better chance of being around people you know better than in other areas.

This also means you can barter with people in the neighborhood for items you need without having to worry so much about them pulling a weapon and just taking your supplies and giving you nothing in return.

If you do form a group with people local to you, you can even put certain systems into place. For example you could set up watches where a couple of people take it in turns to stand watch and warn of any outsiders that are approaching. You can also set up scouting or scavenging teams that go out together and either try to find supplies or communicate with other survivors and trade supplies.

If you decide to bug out, you will lose this potential support system. You can obviously take people with you but you won't have as large of a group as if you stayed put.

When encountering other people in a bug out situation, you greatly increase the chance of hostility seeing as they will not know you at all. In your local area the chance is reduced due to the likely hood of people knowing or recognizing you and this alone will greatly reduce the chance of dangerous confrontations.

5. EXPOSURE

If you do decide to bug out and leave the comfort of your home you will of course be exposed to the elements. This may not seem so bad, a bit of camping out in the woods never killed anyone right?

Well if the situation becomes very drawn out, having a decent roof over your head will be far more beneficial and will improve morale dramatically. Most people probably think that living in a makeshift shelter or a tent wouldn't be too bad, but you will soon start to miss the comforts of home very badly indeed.

Even if you make a good quality shelter or have an expensive tent you can use, the weather will still cause you problems when you're not in a house.

This problem is magnified significantly if you have anyone with you who is less physically capable of dealing with this type of environment. Such as the elderly or someone with a physical disability of some kind.

As for Mother Nature. When you're not in a strong, sturdy structure that provides a barrier against her barrage of abuse, things can get a bit tricky. For starters, even high winds can cause a big problem. Not only by un-securing tents and tarps but also, seeing as most people would be headed into wooded areas, by bringing down trees on top of shelters that offer the people inside no protection from the impact.

Rain will obviously be problematic and so will low temperatures. When you're out in these conditions you will probably be regretting leaving those strong walls and leak-proof roof.

I think most people would be surprised at how unprepared they are for living out in the elements after an entire lifetime being almost completely sheltered from them by living in a comfortable modern home.

Also you will probably have things like board games and books in your home which will help occupy your mind. I would imagine most people would be extremely appreciative of any form of entertainment in a drawn out, bleak survival situation if it goes on from long enough. Anything that will take your mind off of the situation and offer some light relief will surely help you get through the situation you are in for as long as it takes to blow over. In the woods, without any form of entertainment you may begin to overthink things and the paranoia and feeling of helplessness is going to sink in far more quickly.

Some people may argue that out in the woods, life would be far more interesting and your mind would in fact be far more occupied due to all of the day to day task you would have to carry out in order to survive. In reality the novelty of surviving in the woods would wear off very quickly, especially when you know there is no choice. Those day to day survival routines such as foraging for anything you can find to sustain yourself and gathering fire wood or water will quickly turn into monotony and sap your morale even more.

It one thing going out into the woods and camping out for a weekend or rambling about for fun. It's another when your life depends on it and you have to do it every day with no end in sight. In that situation I think most people would quickly regret leaving their comfortable bed, leak proof roof and strong walls.

Steve Rayder

6. SUPPLY STOCKPILES

If you're bugging out, you can't realistically take a whole lot with you. If you have a decent sized vehicle you may be able to fit a lot in but then you're going to need petrol which is going to be either in very short supply or largely non-existent.

So unless you have enough fuel to get you safely to your bug out location, you're not going to be able to take a lot with you at all. Also, the roads are likely to be blocked anyway. And even if you do get there, someone may find you and you may have to move those supplies.

At home you can stockpile and protect your supplies far more easily than you could if you were on the road. If you're bugging out, at some point it's fairly likely you will need to travel on foot meaning you can only take what you can carry.

Then if you get injured or you're weak because you haven't been eating enough then you will be able to carry even less.
So by staying at home you will have everything you need, you don't need to move it anywhere or use up precious calories lugging it about.

I'm not just talking about food here either. There's water, tools, clothing, shelter building equipment, medical supplies, etc. If you're at home then it's all in one place.

So, I want to talk a bit about food and water stockpiles. There is two main ways to stockpile food. The first is very simple, just buy more of what you eat. So you're just buying standard canned and dried packets food that you would eat on a day to day basis and as you eat into your supplies you keep buying more so you always have a stockpile. That way you will always have a decent amount of extra food in case you need it.

The second way is my personal favorite. For this method you simply to buy extremely long life food and leave it for if an emergency situation occurs. There are specialist canned foods you can buy that will last for 30 years or more. So this way you don't have to worry about constantly replenishing your supplies and you just buy it and leave it for when you need it. How you do it is completely up to you.

Something that is great to keep in your stockpile are foods that you can eat cold straight out of the can if you need to, the reasons for this are obvious as fuel for making fire and water for rehydrating or cooking will be limited.

Dried beans and rice are also fantastic for long term storage and as they are dry and therefore much lighter and more compact than canned food. Beans and rice may not sound like the most appealing thing ever but it does sustain life. You can life off of them for a long time so I would say this is the best starting point if you're just getting your stockpile going.

White rice is the best as far as rice goes because it lasts much longer than brown rice. If you're thinking about storing flour it should last for about 10 years but if you store wheat instead it will last indefinitely.

I would also recommend keeping sugar, salt and spice stockpiles as they will also keep things interesting and help keep morale up.

Your will to live will be sapped pretty quickly eating plain beans and rice 3 times a day!

You can also mix some of your canned food with some rice and beans so there is ways of making things a bit more interesting for yourself. This will also help you transition into a diet that consists mainly of just rice and beans, which can be hard for the body to get used to if it's a sudden switch.

I see a lot of preppers saying they have these big stockpiles of MRE's. It stands for Meals Ready to Eat. The thing is, you shouldn't be eating them for an extended period of time. They are also really expensive and heavy too if you did need to transport them anywhere. So personally, I don't see the point in them.

So how much food should you keep? Well for most standard natural disasters, a month's supply of food should be sufficient to see you through. I think everyone should keep this whether you're a prepper or not. If you want to keep more then that's entirely up to personal preference.

To store your non-tinned foods you can of course leave them in the bag they came in. But if you want to extend the life of your food for as long as possible, you should get some Mylar bags.

One you have transferred your food into the bags you will then need to add an oxygen absorber. As a guide a 2000cc oxygen absorber will be ideal for a 5 gallon bag. Side note: don't bother with oxygen absorbers for salt and sugar as there really is no need.

Mylar bags can be sealed with something like a standard clothes iron as the two sides of the bag will melt together and form an airtight barrier keeping your food fresh for as long as possible. You can then store these bags as they are and label them with a sharpie or you can put the bags into buckets with lids to ensure they don't get punctured and to add an extra airtight seal.

As for water, if you're being careful with it, you will need about 2 gallons of water a day as minimum for general use. The CDC recommends storing 150 gallons for a 30 day period for just one person. That's a not typo, 150 gallons. Now the water may be still running for a time in a disaster and you can always set up systems to catch rain water so it's probably not essential to keep that much. But I would suggest keeping as much as you can.

Unfortunately that water you have stored won't stay fresh forever so you're going to need to be able to make it safe to drink when the time comes.

I would recommend getting a specialist water filter such as Berkey which will do a fantastic job on giving you clean drinking water without boiling from any water source. The reason I recommend this is because you can purify any type of water with it including rain water, old tap water and even water from ponds and streams and swimming pools.⏺

7. GETTING FROM A TO B

Another thing that is important to remember and that I touched on in the last chapter is that transportation will be a real problem. The scenes you see in post-apocalyptic movies of roads being blocked by cars is actually a fairly likely scenario. Traffic jams will become a real problem as people start to head for greener pastures that they will probably never find en masse.

This not only means the roads will be blocked and cars won't be moving, but also road rage and theft could even be a danger whilst everyone is trying to leave urban areas and stuck there with all of their supplies like sitting ducks.

People could easily hold you up with a gun or a knife if you're stuck in a traffic jam seeing as you can't get away, this becomes more likely if you have stocked your car full of valuable supplies that are on show through the windows.

You can safely assume that city centers will be almost completely blocked with people either fleeing or trying to get home within hours of a disaster or an attack occurring. Being in a vehicle on the streets during this time could turn out to be a very bad move. If a storm or a hurricane was the cause of the disaster then there is also a very high likely hood that the roads will be blocked with fallen trees and telephone masts.

A large scale earthquake could cause damage to roads and make them unpassable. For those of you who are worried about a super volcano, ash can render any airborne form of transportation useless but it can also cause visibility to reach the point where driving isn't possible at all without crashing. Also if the ash if a foot or two foot deep you won't be able to drive in that even when it has settled.

There is even the possibility that your car could break down. Or there could be debris on the road causing you to get a couple of punctures.

So bugging out in a vehicle with large amounts of supplies may not be as simple as you think for a lot of reasons. I'm not saying not to have a bug out plan or a vehicle to transport supplies, I'm just saying you should only bug out if you absolutely need to. As I have mentioned in another one of my books, I actually have a bicycle that I can use if I need to. They have a surprisingly large weight capacity and obviously don't need an energy source to power them other than your legs which is great in a survival situation.

In fact they can provide electricity if you get a generator for you back wheel. These generators can fully charge an iphone in under an hour too so it's actually a surprisingly decent amount of electric they provide you with.

Just remember that on a bike you are exposed. Unless you take a route where they can't follow you then you can be caught by anyone in a car or van for example. People will probably try and steal your bike too if you're one of the only people who has had the bright idea of cruising through a traffic jam on it. So there are drawbacks. But at least you will be able to navigate roads when the traffic has stopped and you can always try and steer clear of populated areas.

If you wanted to stealth up your bike for bugging out you should consider spraying it dark brown, green or black. Matt paint will help stop the paintwork from reflecting light. You can also use camo-wrap tape to cover the frame and give a really nice tactical look. As for the noise of the rear wheel, you can actually buy silent hubs so that the annoying clicking sound of the freewheel won't draw any attention to you. If you do this and travel at night with no lights or reflectors, you will have a much better chance of getting from A to B without being spotted.

The point really though is that being on the road without rule of low will be a big problem. So staying put unless you really have to will be the best option.

8. REASONS TO LEAVE

Of course there may be reasons why you have no other choice but to leave your home.

As I mentioned in the introduction, your home may become extremely damaged in whatever disaster that caused things to get to this point.

There are other reasons you may need to leave however. For example, if things get really bad and one of your family members passes away in your home, I would imagine most people wouldn't want to stay there and deal with being in that place for any longer than they had to.

If there are gangs raiding nearby town that you have heard about and you think they might be headed your way, if you have no real way of defending yourself then it may well be best to get all of your things and leave before they get to you rather than trying to defend yourself against them.

You may also find it hard to gather large amounts of water in an urban environment. Of course you can dig shallow wells and create systems to gather rain water but this isn't always going to yield enough in some dryer areas and in the summer months especially. In these cases you will need to move closer to a river or another water source.

Also food will almost certainly become a problem at some point seeing as there is only so much food you can store. You can always try finding other survivors nearby and trading with them for some food. But if you're in a woodland or forest area at least you can try to hunt, fish and forage. Even if there are other people doing the same thing, it's better than sitting at home and starving to death because you have used all of your supplies.

Steve Rayder

9. REFUGEE CAMPS

Even in an extreme disaster situation there is a possibility that there is still some kind of law or government that will try to maintain rule and set up camps for the survivors.

If you leave your home and go to one of these places it's going to be rough. There will be thousands of people. You will be in horrible conditions sleeping shoulder to shoulder with people you don't know on makeshift beds.

Fights will probably break out, food will be in short supply. There will probably be certain people at these places who are willing to prey on others that can't defend themselves and take what little they have from them.

I would imagine these places will be a lot like being in prison. The officials will just see you as one of the inmates and will treat you like cattle. Just another one of the masses that they need to deal with. They won't care about any personal issues you may be having as everyone else will be telling them about the same thing.

If you own or manage to find a weapon, it will be taken from you because they're not going to let you in with it. The same thing will more than likely go with knives and multitool. Any food supplies you have will be taken from you and distributed among everyone else. They will be perfectly entitled to do this as soon as martial law is declared.

So not only will you be in a pretty dire situation, you will also have no weaponry or supplies left if things go bad at the camp.

I personally would avoid refugee camps at all costs. I would first of all try to stay at home until I couldn't any longer. Then if the time came, I would bug out. Then if I was facing death, I would have no choice but to seek out a camp. But it would only be if all else failed.

The main thing that happens by going to one of these places is that you put your life completely in their hands. You have no say in your fate any longer.

For the elderly or the weak this may well be the best option for them as at least they will have some kind of protection due to the guards and security they have stationed there.

Another thing you need to keep in mind about refugee camps is that sickness can spread very quickly seeing as so many people are crammed into a small space and proper sanitation isn't possible. This becomes especially problematic if the disaster that caused this situation was some kind of pandemic for example.

By bugging in and staying at home, you know the people around you and if they're sick you can take the proper precautions to make sure it doesn't spread. You can have much better control over sanitation in general too.

I think a lot of people would head to a camp if a disaster were to occur because they're not prepared for a disaster and also we have a society that is over reliant on a system that tells them what to do and think. It's not really their fault they just became too safe in modern society and believed that nothing could go wrong.

But for you, reading this book, you will have prepared. So I would say steer clear until the time comes that you have no other choice.

Steve Rayder

10. SANITATION

Now I think most people realize that there would be a point, if society did really go down the pan, where electricity, gas and water would stop working.

This obviously causes a lot of issues and the lack of running water would make washing a problem. But the thing most people don't consider or maybe understand the implications of fully is that the sewage would also not be working.

With the amount of people in urban and suburban locations producing the amount of sewage that we do, sanitation is going to become a huge issue to say the least.

I expect some people will just throw their sewage out into the gutter or drains. People who live in flats and apartments would most likely have to dig a communal latrine on the communal grounds. If you have a garden you will have to make your own. Side note, you should be keeping large quantities of toilet roll with your other supplies if you don't already.

As for washing, I would recommend keeping a solar shower in case you ever need it. If you haven't heard of a solar shower before, you just fill them with water and hang them in the sun so it can heat the water inside.

You can keep a supply of spare soap, shampoo, shower gel etc. Another advantage of bugging in is that you will have these things already.

I would also recommend keeping spare tooth paste and mouth wash and spare detergent for washing your clothes.

Steve Rayder

11. HOME DEFENSE

The topic of home defense is obviously subject to the type of property and environment you live in. But there are a few things we can all consider no matter where we live.

You may already have an alarm or a CCTV system installed but without electric they obviously won't be working. Also, even if they did work, in a disaster situation there may be no one to respond even if they alarm did go off.

So we need to rely on more basic methods of home security. The first thing I want to cover is the humble sign. You can do two things by putting a sign up at your door or at your gate. You can either deter potential robbers or you could make them think you're a more valuable target.

I have seen signs that say, "Warning: Loaded gun kept on premises at all times". Or some people put up National Rifle Association signs. Now that will obviously deter some people but to some others they might try even harder to get in and take the guns. I'm going to leave this one up to you but I personally wouldn't want to stand out in any way so I will not be putting up any signs.

Securing your doors should be a high priority when considering home defense. Surprisingly about 80% of burglaries occur by breaking and entering through the front door. I would highly recommend taking a look at the OnGARD or the Nightlock door braces which are highly effective at securing standard exterior doors such as your front and back door. They are good to have anyway but in a WROL situation they would give you great peace of mind. They work by screwing directly into the floor so they aren't reliant on the door frame holding.

I would also highly recommend getting some Buddybar Door Jammers for securing any interior doors quickly and easily if you need to. They are made from solid steel and they work much like wedging a chair against the door handle but with much more reliability. If you have a couple of these you can help to secure certain areas of your house. This won't hold forever if someone is persistent enough but they will buy you valuable time to grab what you can and get out.

If you have an open porch leading to your front door you can also consider having some gates installed so that people can't come right up to your door and try to break in without getting through the gate first.

As for windows, they are obviously fairly easily smashed. You can however get hurricane shutters to shut off your windows should you need to. This will provide a huge security bonus in a WROL situation as they will also blackout your windows meaning you won't run the risk of attracting anyone with candles or any other form of light during the night.

To help prevent people entering your property in the first place by climbing over your fence or wall you could obviously use some barbed wire but this will draw attention to you. If I was looting and I saw a house with barbed wire around the walls and fence I would instantly assume there was some good stuff in there and get the wire cutters out. If people are desperate enough they will start attacking even the best defended homes. A good way to have the same effect in a very inconspicuous way is to plant thorny climbing plants along the perimeter of your garden. They won't stop intruders completely but they will ensure they can't just quickly and silently jump onto your property.

Probably the best deterrent and form of protection against an intruder in a situation like this is of course a fire arm. If you don't want to keep a gun you could also keep pepper spray instead. If you jump out on someone and hit them in the face with pepper spray it will certainly incapacitate them.

If you live in a country where guns and pepper spray are illegal such as the UK, you can still keep Farb Gel and air rifles without any kind of license. Farb Gel is a bit like pepper spray but without the irritants, it's a criminal identifier that stains skin red for weeks and foams up when it's sprayed. If you spray them in the face this will distract an attacker for long enough for you to try to escape or hit them.

Air rifles are not only good for home defense but they are also good to have in case you need to bug out or hunt small game at any point. Most air rifles are single shot only but you can get semi-automatics that are powered with gas cylinders. If your main priority is home defense then you can also get a semi-automatic air pistol which is better for close quarter's combat. The sight of which will be a potent deterrent for any assailant as they look like real guns. They may not kill someone but they would still do a lot of damage and stop someone in their tracks, especially if you shot them in the head or neck for example.

Another good may of defending your home is to make it look like it's not worth looting. I definitely think it's best to blend in as best as possible. Or, even better, make it look as if your house has already been looted and is not worth even trying.

You can do this by throwing things around the garden to make it look a mess. If you have some black spray paint you can also spray burn marks around your windows and doors to make it look like there was a fire. Obviously you will want to black out your windows so that people can't see you walking around inside, especially at night.

Steve Rayder

12. FINAL THOUGHTS

Well I think that about overs it for this installment of the Preppers Apocalypse Survival Guide! I have added a checklist at the end of this book with all of the things I think you should keep in your home at all times in order to be fully prepared for a bug in situation.

I'm currently giving away a free e-book that I wrote specifically as a thank you for everyone who signs up to my mailing list to find out about future books as I release them. You can get the free book and sign up on my author page at – www.southshorepublications.com/steverayder

If you would also consider taking the time to leave me an honest review on this book on Amazon I would be extremely appreciative of your feedback.

You can also find links to all of my previous books at - http://www.amazon.com/Steve-Rayder/e/B00U0U3Z3E/ or by searching for "Steve Rayder" on Amazon.

Thanks for reading and I will catch you all next time!